26 Angels: Words for a Healing Heart

OUMAR DIENG

26 Angels: Words for a Healing Heart

Copyright © 2013 by Bookbyline.com
info@bookbyline.com

All rights reserved.
ISBN: 1482774208
ISBN-13: 978-1482774207

Dedication

In memory of the victims of Sandy Hook Elementary who won't be forgotten. To the victims of Red Lake Senior High School, Columbine High School, Virginia Polytechnic Institute and all other schools that have endured a tragedy.

CONTENTS

Acknowledgments i

Introduction ii

CHAPTER 1: ANGELS 1

I am Sandy Hook 4

Angels of Sandy Hook 6

Twenty Kids 7

26 Angels 8

Angels in a Cupboard 10

Tell Me It's Not True 12

26 Angels 13

How Could We Know 14

God's 26 New Angels 15

Hiding 17

Lullaby 20

The River's End 22

Why Me? 24

CHAPTER 2: HEALING 27

I Am Not Naïve 30

Angels, Oh Angels 32

I Lost My Buddy 34

Things Beneath, Things Above 36

CHAPTER 3: CLOSURE 39

Dreams and Life 41

My Dream: Falling Angels 44

Memories 46

Love, Live 47

No Boundaries 49

How Do I Move On 50

We, the 26 Angels 52

Never Harm Children 54

The Right Question 56

About The Author 59

Acknowledgments

I would like to thank the following individuals without whom this book might not have seen the light of day and to whom I am greatly indebted.

To Ana M. Fores Tamayo, Cyril Mukalel, Danielle Wirsansky, Dawn M. Carvalho, Emily Grealish, Evelyn F. Elbe, Ginny Clerget, Glata Grindstaff, Joey Michael Ochoa, Julia Kranenburg, Kirk Dunst, Kyle D. Paul, Lloyd S. Foote, Mark Anthony Grubb, Nancy Jaimes Reyes, Stephanie Kawada and William Sawyers. These poets whose written contributions and participation in this book project are a true testament that altruism is alive and well within our communities.

To Bill Begany who gratefully and masterfully designed the book cover.

To Ann Curry whose tweet of "20 acts of kindness" inspired this book project.

Introduction

On December 14, 2012, my heart sunk when I learned of the Sandy Hook Elementary School shooting. Like many of you, this unfortunate event hit home hard as I thought of my own children. "What if this happened at my son's school?" If this simple thought made my heart skip a beat, I couldn't begin to imagine how the victims' families must have felt.

Drawing from my personal experiences around loss, I remembered how helpful it was to have "the village", those who love and care about us, come together to help in the healing process: the 26 Angels book project was born. In memory of the 26 lives lost that day at Sandy Hook Elementary - 27 lives altogether, poems were collected from authors across the country and compiled in this book in hopes of raising awareness on children's safety in schools and in doing so, give some closure to those who are grieving either directly or indirectly from this tragedy.

This book is not meant to convey a position on the issue of gun violence but rather an appeal to common sense and the recognition of an innate right to safety that every human being, regardless of race or background, aspires to. We will never keep our children safe if we insist on asking the wrong questions. The wrong questions are distractions disguised as legitimate issues that lock our leaders into a vicious circle of indecision spanning administrations.

As fathers, mothers, brothers, sisters, grandparents, uncles and aunts, it is our responsibility to make sure that those we have elected stay focused on the real issues. If there is one thing on which we all agree, it is that our children should be safe. Consequently, the right question, the only question, has to be "How do we keep our children safe?" The answer to this question resides on the floors of our senates and houses with a subtle encouragement from the watchful eyes of all those who could not bear to lose a loved one or see another Sandy Hook.

Meanwhile, let us come together and support all those who have lost a family member so they may grieve with dignity and find the will to go on. Spark a conversation in your communities or through social media with the hashtags: #26Angels and #26AngelsBook.

CHAPTER 1: ANGELS

I am Sandy Hook

I am a son to a woman.
I am a nephew to a man.
I am an uncle to a child.
I am a cousin to a young man.
I am a father to a young son.
So were they.
As I imagine the pain felt, it grows.
I know your pain. I share your pain.
I am Sandy Hook!

It intensifies as I think of the children in my life.
It becomes unbearable as I see their faces.
Young faces, innocent faces, unsuspecting faces!
I find no solace in the words of others.
I find no relieve in the sacred words,
Less the friendly hugs of others.
As I imagine the pain felt, it intensifies.
I know your pain. I share your pain.
I am Sandy Hook!

I swear I am angry. I just am.
I swear I am outraged. I just am.
I swear, by the seven wonders,
Something has to give
Something must give;
Enough is enough!
As I imagine the pain felt, it implodes.
I know your pain. I share your pain.

I am Sandy Hook.
I grieve with Sandy Hook.

Oumar Dieng, Minnesota.

Angels of Sandy Hook

Fly, little angels,
Far away from there.
Fly to where
You will no longer be scared.

Your families will miss you,
And tears will be shed
Over how they can no longer put you to bed.
But up in heaven,
Look down on them and smile
To give them strength for a while.

Oh, little angels,
With halos of gold-
Your smiles were filled with joy
The world could never hold.

Little angels with wings of white,
Eleven days before Christmas, you took flight.
The nation is crying, so many tears shed
And a great many lower their heads.

Julia Kranenburg, Illinois.

Twenty Kids

Twenty lives are wiped away,
Not to see another day.
Twenty families with broken hearts,
And twenty families now, torn apart.
Twenty kids with futures destroyed,
Twenty kids without their toys.
Twenty futures left unwritten.

Now, twenty families without their children.
Twenty moms now cry in pain
For twenty kids who died in vain.
Twenty kids will never know
What it's like to age and grow,
To drive a car, or graduate.

No twenty first kisses
And no twenty first dates.
Twenty less birthdays
And twenty less proms.
Eight less dads,
And twelve less moms.

No twenty weddings
And no twenty first loves.
But now twenty more angels
In heaven above.

Kirk Dunst, Missouri.

26 Angels

26 angels all in heaven now,
Taken before their time.
Never too late to be torn from a mother
Father, brother, sister or friend.

26 faces that smiled and laughed,
With no reason to be sad at the time,
Felt nothing but love towards anyone
Whose pure, undying love would never bend.

26 children have gone amiss,
And though wounds may not heal with time,
We will be there, and we will help one another
To know that, much as we love something, everything ends.

26 families brought closer together,
For now and for all time.
The absence of a loved one tethers
All together, the world, a family, pulsing in the same vein.

26 lives, a treasure beyond measure
Lost to us but for a time,
For when that sleep we finally fall under,
We will be reunited, free to make amends.

26 souls await those who love them
And though this love will not fade with time,
The pain will subside and the memories aflutter
With happiness that once was and will be again.

Joey Ochoa, Texas.

Angels in a Cupboard

It started out, another day
Just like every other.
None ever thought they'd hide to live,
Locked tight inside a cupboard.

Innocent lives forever changed.
One fateful, hateful day.
One man with evil in his heart
Destroyed them in many a way.

Their teacher was so quietly brave.
As these angels, each she hid
And bade them all to remain quiet.
Thank God above they did!

Each life was spared because of her.
She saved them at great cost
For in protecting those dear lambs,
The teacher's life was lost.

A sacrifice so pure and true.
She will never be forgotten
For being a light so warm and clear
In a world that's turned so rotten.

Those little lives can now be lived,
To maybe make great change
In a world so black and cold
They may possibly rearrange.

I know each night when they lie down,
They will forever remember
How their world changed, forever more,
On the 14th of December.

It started out, another day
Just like every other.
None ever thought they'd hide to live,
Locked tight inside a cupboard.

Glata Grindstaff, North Carolina.

Tell Me It's Not True

I dropped you off at school today,
I told you what I always say;
"I love you and be good."
I went to work like every other day,
But a few hours later, nobody knew what to say.

Your presents are still under the tree.
I don't know what to do.
I wish someone would wake me up and tell me it's not true.
I had my sweet Angel for six short years,
But now, it is forever that I will have these tears.
I had big plans for you and me!
There was so much more for you to see.

I know you're safe in Jesus' arms
And He will hold you tight,
But I would give anything to hold you close
If only for just one more night.

Dawn M. Carvalho, Illinois.

26 Angels

On a dark day in December, we will always remember
How 26 angels' souls took flight.
They left behind life, terrible hatred, and strife,
And sailed up to a beautiful Light.

They stopped at the gate, where Jesus did wait.
His big loving arms carried them through.
 He led them to a place, all built by God's grace, the
26 angels had no clue.
Then tears flowed down from Jesus's eyes,
He told them they were in Paradise.
He told them He was always there, among the bullets
flying everywhere.
He was beside each one of them as they died.
He told them He was the bright Light that was by
their side.

Jesus wants everyone to know,
For those who have been left behind,
Down here below,
If a kind, loving life you live,
And have a heart that can forgive,
Then someday God, you will meet,
And your family circle will be complete, forever!

Ginny Clerget, Washington.

How Could We Know

The last supper done and tucked in their beds.
The last time the pillow would cuddle their heads.
A last glance at the tree, the presents and bows.
Their gifts never opened but how could we know?

Tiny hands were washed and breakfast was served.
And thanks be to God was the last prayer they heard.
The last trip to school full of laughter and cheers,
Would end abruptly with screams and with tears.

Swings now hang lonely and pets stare at the place
Looking for the arrival of their friends smiling face.
Unique little voices that filled playgrounds with joy
Won't sing Jingle Bells or play with their toys.

How could we know this was their homecoming day?
Hastened by men's hatred that would take them away.
God's innocent souls that we all loved and adored
Would never leave school or come home anymore.

Mark Anthony Grubb, Virginia.

God's 26 New Angels

Today God got 26 new Angels.
Scared and sad they may be
But they are not alone.
Today God got 26 new Angels
Each different from the last.
One with blonde curls,
One with glasses,
One with two missing teeth.

Today God got 26 new Angels.
They were each frightened, but not alone.
They were together.
They walked up the heavenly staircase in line,
Like they do for lunch, led by their teacher,
Led by their friend.

Today God got 26 new Angels.
Each just as special as the last.
They were wrapped in God's warm embrace,
Held close and loved.
"Don't be afraid my children" He whispered.

Today God got 26 new Angels.
Each was given a set of wings.
They saw family and friends,
Lost pets and other kids
And a glorious feast just the same.

Today God got 26 new Angels.
And each made sure to look down from the clouds,

To watch their families in sorrow and in pain.

Today God's 26 new Angels
Cried with their families as they watched.
God's 26 new Angels played in the fields,
Rolled in the grass, ate chocolate for breakfast,
And had pancakes for lunch.

Today God got 26 new Angels
Who spent the day catching up.
Who spent the day playing with God's other children.

Today God got 26 new Angels.
But tomorrow we won't forget.

Emily Grealish, North Carolina.

Hiding

1, 2, 3
The race is on.
Feet slap the pavement, hands shoving, mouths snickering,
And then comes the moment where you fall to your knees,
Or duck into the shadows,
Or climb out of sight.

9, 10, 11
Your heart races in your ears.
Your breathing is fast, fast, fast,
And you try to make it slow,
Because they'll hear you,
They'll *hear* you.

24, 25, 26
You must be silent, must be still.
And as you wait,
As you are motionless,
The quiet calms you.
You are peaceful in your solitude.
You are content in your vanishing place.
You are invisible to all,
And it is good.
Ready or not, here I come!

But then the game is different.
The laughter dies down,
The teachers are playing.

And the game is inside.
A game inside?
Is that allowed?

1, 2, 3
The world explodes.
Feet hit the carpet, hands shoving, mouths screaming,
And you fall to your knees,
Or duck into the shadows,
Or climb out of sight.

9, 10, 11
Your heart races in your ears.
Your breathing is fast, fast, fast,
And you try to make it slow,
Because he'll hear you,
He'll *hear* you.

24, 25, 26
You must be silent, must be still.
But your quiet is so loud,
And your stillness is full of runnings.
You are frightened in your vanishing place.
You feel caught, feel exposed.
This is like your game, isn't it?
And yet, it's not.

You are left behind;
And you are still afraid.
But when you shut your eyes,
Can't you see them?

It's a playground,
Much like yours,
But it stretches on forever.

1, 2, 3
They are different now;
Not like you remember.
They are bright, and soft, and quick.
As they run to hiding places,
Their feet hardly touch the ground.

9, 10, 11
The teachers play as well,
And they seem happy to be playing,
Like children.

24, 25, 26
You are left on the empty playground.
You are not allowed to play,
Because you are dull,
And hard, and slow.
But when the day is right,
You will be different.
Like them.
And you will be the one to cry:
Ready or not, here I come!

Evelyn F. Elbe, Illinois.

Lullaby

That malignant spell awoke me
To macabre dreams of death:
And as I watched uncannily
His beastly body raptured,
A child grew wild,
Neanderthal beginnings wrapped
In sordid ecstasies.
A darkness grew,
Enveloped wild glass jungles
And the pitfalls numbered burrs,
Bleeding my aching body
As I stumbled far far into the night.

All light receded,
Becoming frenzied fantasy of music
Lumbering in fatal destiny,
And I cried on in agony,
A wounded dying animal shrieking
In that mocking silence
Of a world gone mad.
That hanging head,
Medusa's locks untarnished,
Falls to the ground
Where slivering snarling snakes
Hiss their poison
And sting that beastly child.

Death strikes,
Pounds pistols shooting
In a wild attack
And that boy is dead:
Beast-child of fantasy retrieved
From webbed denial,
Dead bleeding throat and head hanging...
Wake, my child, awake...

Ana M. Fores Tamayo, Texas.

The River's End

Land I shall never feel
For I row in my grief.
I see not the river's end;
I look for the end
But I row on the river forever.

On the river's edge,
I see little children at play.
Their innocence so pure,
Their eyes so unchanged
By the evil of our world.

Down the river I row.
The little children follow me
Along the river's edge
For they see not the world's bad,
But all the good they see.

Flowing down the river,
My eyes glance back
To see the children follow.
No longer they follow.
No longer I see them.

I look up into the sky.
The sun shines so bright.
I hear the children's laughter.
They brighten the sky
For no longer do they see evil.

No longer do they know

The world and its evil.
They know nothing but good.
Forever shall they know good,
Forever they live in innocence.

And down the river I flow.
I still see not the river's end
For my grief for the children
It knows no end as the river.
And forever I flow downriver.

Kyle D. Paul, Florida.

Why Me?

The old man sat in his big oak chair,
Blind eyes staring out at the sea.
He pictured the things he had never beheld
And his heart cried out, "why me?"

The young boy sat in his new wheel chair
Heartsick his life would be,
The life of a cripple with feeling gone,
And he wept as he thought, "why me?"

Twenty children, six leaders with families dear
Fell to earth with a bullet's decree,
And their families cried out with broken hearts
Why them, dear Father, "why me"?

The Savior looked down with love in his heart,
Understanding the loss they would see
As He remembered the day on the cross
When he too had cried out "why me?"

And his father had answered, "why you indeed?
Earth's road is a difficult test.
Some of my children can't carry the load."
I've had to determine my best."

"To these now have come the difficult task –
Brought on by a wicked one.
With heavy heart I've allowed it to be
Like with you my beloved son."

The Savior then smiled and spoke with love

To give peace and power to see,
That their cross, though hard and their journey rough,
In their hearts they're much like me.

"The day will come, I promise you that,
When you will be able to see,
And then you can say as I have said
"Thank you Lord for the peace you give me. "

Lloyd S. Foote, Arizona.

CHAPTER 2: HEALING

I Am Not Naïve

I am not naïve, I am trusting.
I am not little, I am growing.
It is not safe here but If the sky is falling,
Let it be my calling.

This chaotic reign of terror
Sees grownups in disarray;
Vernacular so unfamiliar.
The balance of trust is in error,
Feelings in shambles hidden in an array
Opposite the spectrum of circles linear.

Time stands still
As celestial beings present,
Invisible to the untrained eye,
Amuse the children bewildered.
There is no past, future or present,
As senses come to a standstill.
Elevated in pairs identical and ordered,
Soaring over the horizon with wings of a buckeye.

A sordid yet soothing peace overcomes,
Extended from the wingtips of my protectors,
Formal and de-cloaked in the nick of time.
Bright is the guiding hand that welcomes
Pure auras mystically shielded against persecutors.
Young minds witness the sight of a lifetime.

I am not naïve, I believe in the unseen.
I am not lost, I am in a better place.

Now I glide proud, alongside prophets unforeseen
On a monotheistic dimension, mankind's original birthplace.

Oumar Dieng, Minnesota.

Angels, Oh Angels

I woke to find you in your bed.
I could never bear to convince myself,
Not even for a moment that you are now gone.
They say everything happens for a reason
What kind of monster, what kind of evil?
For what vile reason would one dare?

Angels, oh Angels
Where are you now?
Whisper to me, tell me you can see me.
Assure me that you are OK.
Is it true you are in a better place?
Are you now one with the Milky Way?

Angels, oh Angels
I imagine you celestial companions,
Touched with an essence omnipresent.
Two archangels guiding each of your paths
As you transcend planes of existence
Unimaginable by us, common mortals.

Angels, oh Angels
In this realm,
Your words are thoughts.
Your thoughts are whispers,
Ever so gently echoing across worlds
Beyond the fragile membrane of live.

Angels, oh Angels
Cradled in a blanket of joy

Amid a divine city of light
Where rainbows flow like
Silky waterfalls bread in mists of serenity.
A restful dwelling for a chosen few.

Oumar Dieng, Minnesota.

I Lost My Buddy

I followed you everywhere
Up and down the stairs.
Where you went, I went.
Where you slept, I slept
Happy and nonchalant.
Always claiming a portion of your bed
Always demanding a piece of your affection.
But today, you are not in your bed.

Search for you I shall.
Paw on, paw off. Paw on, paw off.
I am here!

You are not in your living room chair.
You know, the one I let you sit on!
My instincts dictate that I find you.
My propensity to gravitate towards you
Should aid in solving this mystery.

On with the chase, nose against the floor.
Paw on, paw off. Paw on, paw off.
I am here!

You are not in your parent's bedroom.
Yet there is a picture of you
Frozen in a joyous smile.
As I go on, I tap into our bond.
This bond that unites us is unbreakable.
Like the chains of a titanic anchor,
It is indomitable, priceless and unrelenting.

It guides my senses into the world of angels.

On with the search, ears in the air.
Paw on, paw off. Paw on, paw off.
I am here!

I have been looking in the wrong place.
The realm of angels is where I will find you.
Knowing you are OK has soothed my beastly soul.

I am jasper the cat and I lost my buddy.

Oumar Dieng, Minnesota.

Things Beneath, Things Above

I have faith. Always have.
I accept the implication that the unseen is unknown
Whilst some needed a miracle to believe,
A gaze at the starry heaven's dawn sufficed for me

I hear the tickle induced laughter.
My eyes ache at the sight of this room.
The deafening silence is, oh so cruel.
Stabbing my heart in continuous perpetuity.
It is numbing my core being at its roots.

Things Beneath, things above.
My thoughts wander as I wonder.
One cannot toss seeds and count them mid-air.
Three people cannot wrestle,
Though two are stronger than one.
Seemingly senseless thoughts as these,
Distract me from the reality
That my child's bed will now remain empty.

I feel the light touch of innocence.
I see that angelic face, once a baby.
I remember the first steps, the first words.
Memories forever anchored in my heart.
Memories, now precious, to hold on to.

Things beneath, mysterious and unknown
An unknown reluctantly embraced.
Things above, hopeful like heaven.

Heaven. A good place to rest these memories.
Heaven. A good place for you to rest.
Heaven. Your new room, your new home.

Oumar Dieng, Minnesota.

CHAPTER 3: CLOSURE

Dreams and Life

A baby chortles,
With delight and smiles aglow,
In blue fields of dreams.

He awakens to
Explore the world of vivid
Images and friends.

The child, so flawless,
Frolics in the wondrous awe
Of nature sublime.

Mastering the art
Of tying his shoelaces,
He chatters with joy.

Reveling with love,
His parents and siblings share
A bond unmeasured.

With family pride,
And community values,
He learns social skills.

His mom with happy
Tears ponders his growth
So remarkable.

His dad with broad smiles,
At dusk loves to pitch and catch

With a vibrant son.

His siblings gather
Round to play Monopoly,
Laughter warms the room.

With spring comes new birth,
Splashy colors in meadows,
Cheery chirps of birds.

Summer brings swim suits
And barbeques to the fore,
Joyful times for all.

With fall comes a change,
A brisk wind, red and gold leaves,
Splendor in nature.

Winter brings black ice
And treacherous conditions
Veil of evil lurks.

Families shattered,
Community unraveled,
Horror, senseless acts.

Let the past remain
Always there in history.
Ne'er forget to learn.

Treasure memories,
Raucous laughter, sunny smiles,
Brilliant childhood.

The sun always shines.
After the rain, there is hope
For a better day.

Not the brevity
Of life regret, but love only
Now a job well done.

Your children will stand
For the beauty of mankind
And new hope for us.

Let us move forward
Toward a better tomorrow,
Unmarred and hopeful.

Stephanie Kawada, California.

My Dream: Falling Angels

Some Dreams...I never want to be awake.
I pray the night never ends, leaving the stars to shine forever.
Some Dreams...I never want the day to break.
I know their torment moments would haunt me forever.

Some say the remnants of the past
Make joyous pearls in the brain-folds for the present.
To me it is the reflections of memories from the future.
Breadcrumbs dropped, deceiving elusive realities to come.

Wingless Angels falling from the heavens,
Drenching the clouds on their way in blood.
Oceans merging in rages, submerging the mountains.
Tears from the skies causing the rivers to flood.

I feel I'm just a thought, I'm lost in someone's mind,
Gathering pain for unknown losses to come by.
I drift in the wind, a sparrow amongst the dragons
Waiting to be swallowed by stark naked skies.

My eyes, staring beyond the rain clouds to see the impending.
My heart, a candle unnoticed, burns in the day light.
My face leans forward, blending tears with last raindrops falling.
I hear a whisper from within, powering my spirit.

You are not alone, foregone are the days forlorn.
Pain in your soul will never ever be in vain.
Together our hearts will beat for us to move on.
Together we will share our grief and pain.

While my ears listen to the song of comfort
Like the tender breeze that kisses to bloom the rose buds,
My heart lingers to carry the fragrance of tranquility.
Angels circle above turning fallen wings to colorful clouds.

Cyril Mukalel, Minnesota.

Memories

There stand the walls we thought would last.
With tears, our struggles.
With the days,
The tasks have grown a bit
Lonesome.

Have we lost the "touch"?
It seems light has faded in the matters.
But with our heart beating, we know it will last.

I called her a daughter.
I called him a son.
His memory's my keeper
Of what is to come.

Should we worry for tomorrow?
Should we place a lock on time?
Whatever comes from this occurrence,
May there tears become mine.

May the hearts of the children guide us.
It is them that we left behind,
When growing up seemed harmless.
When society seemed as the only guide.

Let us remember them, not in our silence,
But in the words with which they'd like to have.
May love recover its purpose.
To all, with love.

Nancy Jaimes Reyes, Illinois.

Love, Live

The divine cry of the word bird
Flutters into my ear,
Spiraling ever downward
As I defend against the impending
Death Of the sunrise.

I take the prophet's
Final revelations right out of that
Sleazy, uneasy motel night stand
And thumb through the pages.
There is no perfect ending,
I have to got get and love live my way out;
Only I have the power to employ.

All those lessons learned
From after school specials,
Eyes melting out as the glare scorches
The retinas from a mere three inch distance,
As nose pressed, fingertips rest
On the plasma of the screen.

Savage does the war cry ring as the
Ding a ling goes off after the vibration's sting.
Front pocket trying to strangle the fight
Before it can really begin but it cannot.
Once the gauntlet is raised, the face slapped, the scarf wrapped,
Thumb wars are the only battles
In which I can win.

Salvage the discarded cross from the grime,
Chewed up by the dog.
Thrust away that pomegranate craving;
The balance of flavors is wrong.
It's not an exact science that Mother Nature has,
It's a disease.

Use those prayers as book ends,
Shelving what I truly want
For What I think I want.
Let myself ferment into the sweetness
Bred in a suburban wasteland.
But I can scrub rub my way out,
If only I am ready to shed that skin.

Danielle Wirsansky, Florida.

No Boundaries

There are no boundaries of life in this age;
Just open your mind of empty space.
Learn the knowledge of wisdom through school and books;
As you just can't depend on your looks.
Use your best judgment to follow through.

The future is upon us,
It's all up to you.
If you reach a dead end,
Then start over again.

A day is a day; a year is a year;
Time is one thing you shouldn't fear.
You will succeed one of these days.
Whatever goal you're trying to reach,
I'll wish you luck, as this is the way;
Just try to make the best of your day.

William Sawyers, California.

How Do I Move On

What if
Every child is told the story of their lives,
Their first steps, their first word, their first kiss,
What they will do, what they will become
And even when they will pass on?

What if
All this knowledge is lost, erased before birth?
But somehow nature finds a way.
So, we remember bits and pieces, snippets
Of our future lives.

What if
Before passing on, throughout our lives,
We give "gifts" to those we love?
Imperceptible yet routine gifts
Prompted by faint remembrances
Of our destiny.

What if
These gifts in the memories made,
In the silly things we did,
In the life lessons we learned,
Are the embodiment of the essence,
The main mast to hold on to
Amidst the rough seas of grief
And the stormy winters to come?

What if
Moving on is to honor and cherish this essence?

Though nothing is certain,
The love you still feel is as tangible
As the will, the duty to go on.

Oumar Dieng, Minnesota.

We, the 26 Angels

One with time and space.
Eternal in memories.
Inhabitants of a heavenly place.
Unimaginable in our wildest stories
Is this soothing peace wrapped in grace.

We, the 26 Angels
We project onto you,
When you plant a seed.
We project onto you,
When you do a sincere deed.
We project onto you,
When you take the high road.
We project onto you,
When you save a helpless toad.

We, the 26 Angels
Wish for you to live, fearless.
To laugh again, out loud.
To imagine silly shapes from a cloud.
To run free on the grass, shoeless.
To show that crooked smile, proud.
To walk and use confidence as your shroud.

We, the 26 Angels
Ask that you fight not your emotions.
Go to the mountain top
Where the sky is within reach.
Scream to shed your condemnations
For what you feel will not drop

Till you move beyond the tribulations.

So go on and do that which was left unfulfilled.
As we, the 26 angels, would have.

Oumar Dieng, Minnesota.

Never Harm Children

Never harm children.
For most, this phrase reverberates
On the inner walls of our minds
Echoing ever so loudly
As a moral firewall to our actions,
The main root to the tree of our humanity.

Never harm children.
A commandment steadfast and indomitable.
It is the loud voice of our conscience,
It defines the dichotomy of human versus animal.
When it is set aside, throughout recorded history,
The most shameful moments of humankind occur.

Never harm children.
This tragedy is an infamy,
A burden that should forever haunt,
Like the ghost of our fears within.
It is a microscopic black hole
On the fabric of our mores
And societal pillars already fragile.

Never harm children.
This is neither a mere phrase
Nor a philosophical summation,
Rather it is the seed of future minds,
The ones destined to the helm of a generation
That will leap into the next step in human evolution

The choice is clear;

Sit tranquil and observe mistakes of the past
Morph into poison ivy and induce an itchy wound,
A self inflicted lesion to our future.
Let us dare to be active hopefuls
Who stand tall for those without a voice.
Never harm children, protect them instead.

Oumar Dieng, Minnesota.

The Right Question

Every minute, tragedy strikes somewhere in the world.
The earth quakes often.
Meteors fall from the sky.
Tsunamis rush towards populated beaches.
Fires rage on hillsides, scorching hopes away.

When mother earth lashes out,
We understand and accept it.
Our leaders outshine one another
To mend that which was dismantled.

Yet we watch as they muddy an easy decision
By asking all the wrong questions,
So they can drag their feet
And boot the can down the murky path.

You see. There is but one question,
The only question we should ponder:
How do we keep the children safe?
To ask any other is to filibuster
The resolution of our lifetime.
I know of no existential soul
Who would want children in harm's way.
This is a mere universal truth.

The voice of the people in uproar
Shall rise in protest to see
Demagogues' words put to action
And slight the peripheral brouhaha

That should not take center stage.
Only then would the question,
The right question, be asked.

Oumar Dieng, Minnesota.

About The Author

Oumar Dieng, an avid blogger, a web designer and founder of Bookbyline.com. He has been writing poems for over twenty years, winning his first poetry prize at the age of sixteen. He lives in Minnesota with his wife and three children.

Made in United States
North Haven, CT
20 September 2022